LUIGI
BOCCHERINI
CONCERTO
IN B♭ MAJOR

MAX
BRUCH
KOL NIDREI

for

VIOLONCELLO

and

ORCHESTRA

SUGGESTIONS FOR USING THIS MMO EDITION

WE HAVE TRIED to create a product that will provide you an easy way to learn and perform these pieces with a full orchestra in the comfort of your own home. The following MMO features and techniques will reduce these inflexibilities and help you maximize the effectiveness of the MMO practice and performance system:

Because it involves a fixed accompaniment performance, there is an inherent lack of flexibility in tempo. We have observed generally accepted tempi, but some may wish to perform at a different tempo, or to slow down or speed up the accompaniment for practice purposes. You can purchase from MMO specialized CD players and recorders which allow variable speed while maintaining proper pitch. This is an indispensable tool for the serious musician and you may wish to look into purchasing this useful piece of equipment for full enjoyment of all your MMO editions.

Where the performer begins a movement *solo* or without an introduction from the accompanying instrument, we have provided a set of subtle taps before each piece as appropriate to help you enter with the proper tempo.

We want to provide you with the most useful practice and performance accompaniments possible. If you have any suggestions for improving the MMO system, please feel free to contact us. You can reach us by e-mail at *info@musicminusone.com*.

ABOUT THE 'PRACTICE TEMPO' ACCOMPANIMENTS

As an aid during the early stages of learning these pieces, we have created additional 'practice tempo' accompaniments which have been slowed by approximately 20%. This will allow you to begin at a comfortably reduced speed until technique is more firmly in grasp, at which time the full-speed version can be substituted.

3703

CONTENTS

Luigi Boccherini
VIOLONCELLO CONCERTO
IN B-FLAT MAJOR

Max Bruch
KOL NIDREI

ISBN 1-59615-394-6

CONCERTO
for Violoncello *and* Orchestra
B-flat major 𝄢 Si bemolle maggiore

Luigi Boccherini
(1743-1805)

Allegro moderato
Tutti

SOLO CELLO

8

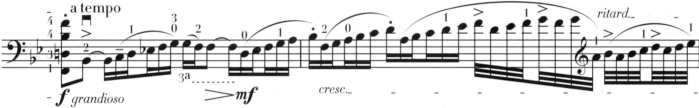

10

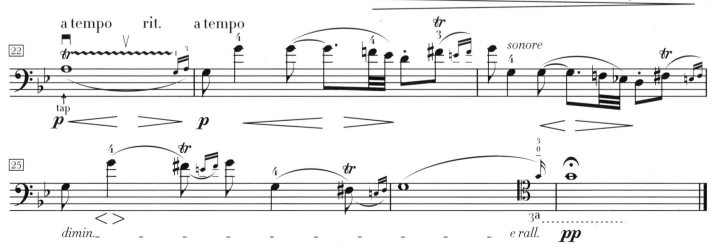

16

MMO 3703

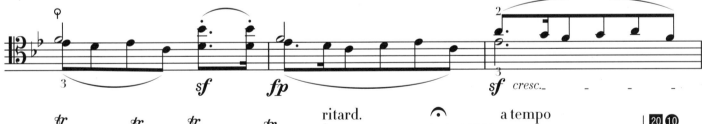

KOL NIDREI

Max Bruch
(1838-1920)
Op. 47

20

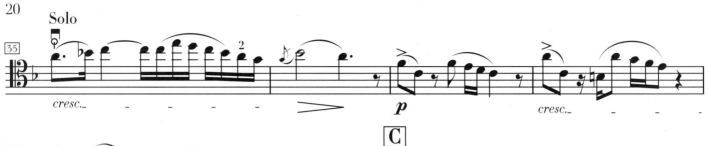

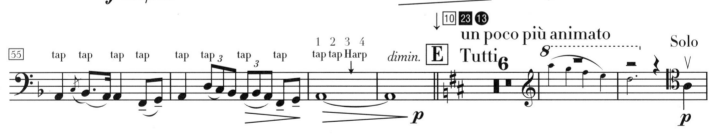

21

Engraving: Wieslaw Novak

BEETHOVEN Piano Trio No. 8 in E-flat major, WoO38 & Trio No. 11 in G major ('Kakadu' Variations), op. 121a MMOCD3710

Alan Shulman (violoncello) - The Vardi Trio: Emanuel Vardi (violin); Edwin Hymovitz (piano) Beethoven's Trio No. 8 is an excellent and beautiful piano trio, beautifully composed in the great composer's inimitable style. Its companion on this MMO edition is the beautiful set of chamber-trio variations on "Ich bin ein Schneider Kakadu," which is justly renowned.

BEETHOVEN String Quartet in A minor, op. 132 (2 CD) MMOCD3713

Evalyn Steinbock (violoncello) - Masako Yanagita (1st violin); Marnie Hall (2nd violin); Linda Lawrence (viola) This beautiful and substantial string quartet is eternally popular amongst chamber music afficionados. Beautiful harmonies, and of course Beethoven's masterful ability to combine the four instruments make it a favorite.

BEETHOVEN Violoncello Sonata in A major, op. 69; TELEMANN Violoncello Duet in B-flat MMOCD3715

Steven Thomas (violoncello) - Steve Isaacson (piano) Beethoven's sonata for violoncello is a staple of the chamber repertoire; Telemann's duet sonata is a feast of 18th-century music at its finest: includes accompaniments for both *primo* and *secondo* parts.

BOCCHERINI Violoncello Concerto No. 9 in B-flat major, G482; BRUCH Kol Nidrei (Adagio on Hebrew Melodies), op. 47 MMOCD3703

Marcy Chanteaux (violoncello) - Stuttgart Symphony Orchestra/Emil Kahn We bring you on this MMO album two pieces from diverse ends of the repertoire: Boccherini's beautiful D-major concerto for violoncello, with its Baroque themes; and Bruch's famous 'Kol Nidrei' with its melding of late Romantic and traditional Hebrew melodies. A great album filled with music to test your abilities in technique and in interpretation.

BOLLING Suite For Violoncello and Jazz Piano Trio MMOCD3706

Dorothy Lawson (violoncello) - Arnold Gross (keyboards); Greg Burrows (drums) This Suite, when first introduced, was performed by Claude Bolling and Jean-Pierre Rampal. It swiftly became the most successful chamber music recording in history with over one-half million copies purchased. Comprised of seven movements, it cleverly exploits the differences between each instrument in a wonderfully effective way. We are delighted to make it available to you, the soloist. Claude Bolling has endorsed this recording.

BRAHMS Double Concerto for Violoncello & Violin in A minor, op. 102 (2CD set) MMOCD3722

Ute Groh (violoncello) - Bojidara Kouzmanova (violin); Plovdiv Philharmonic Orchestra/ Nayden Todorov The famous double concerto, a watershed in the literature for both cello and violin, is now available in a magnificent MMO edition. This majestic work is filled with flowing melody and Brahms' groundbreaking and imaginative use of the two instruments with the orchestra. A summit in the repertoire.

C.P.E. BACH Violoncello Concerto in A minor, Wq170/H432 MMOCD3702

Marcy Chanteaux (violoncello) - Stuttgart Festival Orchestra/Emil Kahn A beautiful baroque concerto for violoncello by Carl Philipp Emanuel Bach, youngest son of J.S. Bach. We can't recommend this gorgeous work enough--filled with beautiful opportunities for the soloist and a magnificent accompaniment. No baroque enthusiast will want to miss out on this rewarding work.

DVORAK Quintet in A major, op. 81 MMOCD3714

Harriet Wingreen (piano); Manhattan String Quartet The second movement of this beautiful quintet is patterned after the 'Dumka' dance form. Beautiful melodies, wonderful orchestration. A quintet of rare quality. In short, wonderful music!

DVORAK Violoncello Concerto in B minor, op. 104 (2 CD Set) MMOCD3701

Dorothy Lawson (violoncello) - Stuttgart Symphony Orchestra/Emil Kahn Dvorak's famed violoncello concerto was inspired by famed 'cellist/composer Victor Herbert's own violoncello concerti. Dvorak went on to write this, one of the treasured masterpieces of the concerted cello repertoire. An absolute must for any serious 'cellist, and for anyone who loves beautiful music in the Romantic idiom. Sumptuous orchestrations in Dvorak's trademark style, long lyrical lines and beautiful use of the instrument's upper ranges. Wonderful for performer and audience alike.

ELGAR Violoncello Concerto in E minor, op. 85 MMOCD3720

Anatoli Krastev (violoncello) - Plovdiv Philharmonic Orchestra/Nayden Todorov Sir Edward Elgar's magnificent Concerto for Violoncello and Orchestra was a tremendous success when it first appeared on the scene and immediately became a staple of the repertoire. It was a specialty of the late Jacqueline du Pré and was accordingly featured in the 1998 film 'Hillary and Jackie.'

Great Scott! Ragtime Minus You MMOCD3708

Zinn's Ragtime String Quartet The Zinn String Quartet accompany you in this great collection of Joplin Ragtime Quartets. Don't miss it!
Eubie Blake Chevy Chase; **Joplin-Chauvin** Heliotrope Bouquet; **Glover** Hurricane Rag; **Joplin** New Rag; Maple Leaf Rag; The Nonpareil; Stoptime Rag; The Easy Winners; **Lucky Roberts** Music Box Rag; **Tom Turpin** Harlem Rag (two-step)

HAYDN Piano Trios, vol. II: G major (HobXV:25), F-sharp minor (HobXV:26), and F major (HobXV:6) minus Violoncello MMOCD3717

Emanuel Vardi (violin); piano accompaniment More of Haydn's wonderful piano trios for you to accompany. Great fun for any 'cellist from this Classical master.

HAYDN Violoncello Concerto in C major, HobVIIb:1 MMOCD3718

Roman Wiszniowski (violoncello) - Plovdiv Philharmonic Orchestra/Nayden Todorov Franz Josef Haydn's beautiful Concerto in C major for Violoncello and Orchestra is a treat as well as an absolute requirement for any serious 'cellist. Strangely, though, it lay dormant and unknown in a Prague library until it was discovered in 1961 and brought to light after nearly two hundred years! Since its reintroduction it has become one of the most popular of all violoncello concerti, and deservedly so. This concerto, written probably in the mid-1760s while Haydn was Kapellmeister to Prince Esterházy, is filled with splendid, memorable themes perfectly written to showcase the solo instrument against a beautifully and sensitively orchestrated backdrop, all of which come together to illustrate Papa Haydn's mastery of form, melody and orchestration. Its lovely classical charm, beautifully captured here by virtuoso Roman Wiszniowski and the Plovdiv Philharmonic, will enchant you from beginning to end. Then play it yourself with maestro Todorov and the Plovdiv Philharmonic as your accompanists! This MMO learning and performance edition of one of the great classical masterpieces for the violoncello is not to be missed!

HAYDN Violoncello Concerto in D major, HobVIIb:2 MMOCD3719

Roman Wiszniowski (violoncello) - Plovdiv Philharmonic Orchestra/Nayden Todorov Haydn's D-major concerto for violoncello is a wonderfully conceived classical piece, filled with many of Haydn's trademarks. Beautiful music as well as an important piece for every serious 'cellist to learn.

RACHMANINOV Sonata for Violoncello and Piano, op. 19 MMOCD3707

Nancy Green (violoncello) – Frederick Moyer (piano) Rachmaninov's most famous chamber composition is finally available as an MMO edition. Featuring a new, annotated urtext score edited by Nancy Green, this classic of the Romantic literature for violoncello is something no 'cellist will want to be without! Listen to Ms. Green's masterful rendition for study purposes, then perform it yourself with Frederick Moyer as your partner on piano!

RAVEL Piano Trio in A minor   MMOCD3707

Alan Shulman (violoncello) - The Vardi Trio: Emanuel Vardi (violin); Edwin Hymovitz (piano) Written in 1914, Maurice Ravel's piano trio was premiered on 28 January 1915 in Paris, with distinguished pianist Alfredo Casella playing the piano part. Filled with Basque themes and Ravel's unique impressionist effects, the four-movement trio (I. Modéré; II. Pantoum; III. Passacaille; IV. Final) is a wonderful piece which is, in its own way, reminiscent at times of his famous *Gaspard de la Nuit*. Highly recommended for any devotée of the French master.

SCHUBERT Piano Quintet in A major, op. 114, D667 'Forellen-Quintett' or 'Trout Quintet'   MMOCD3721

Harriet Wingreen (piano); The Classic String Quartet Schubert's seminal chamber composition, the Piano Quintet in A major, D667, commonly known as 'The Trout' or 'Die Forelle,' is certainly one of greatest pieces of music ever penned. Its rich textures and lovely melody create an unforgettable musical experience. Its celebration of nature's beauty stems from a summer trip in the Austrian Alps which inspired the young Schubert to rework a song into this complex chamber-piece. Composed of five alternating movements, 'The Trout' uses unique orchestration (substituting a double bass for the second violin) and gives special emphasis to the piano as well. But all the instruments take an equal role, and this may also be a reason for the piece's eternal popularity. 'The Trout' instantly brings to mind the calm serenity of the summer mountain air, and its sparkling melody and gentle poignancy leave a particularly happy feeling in both player and listener. It is a joy-filled piece but at the same time is filled with a serene quality that makes it one of the most exhilarating pieces for any musician to play, and one of the most important compositions for any musician to learn. This Music Minus One edition gives you that opportunity!

SCHUBERT Piano Trio in B-flat major, op. 99, D898 (2 CD Set)   MMOCD3711

Alan Shulman (violoncello) - The Vardi Trio: Emanuel Vardi (violin); Alan Shulman (violoncello); Edwin Hymovitz (piano) Schubert's B-flat piano trio is a beautiful and magnificent work, lyrical in character and truly a gem in the chamber repertoire. Delicacy and thoughtful integration of the three instruments make it a joy to perform.

SCHUBERT Piano Trio in E-flat major, op. 100 (2 CD Set)   MMOCD3712

David Miller (violoncello) - The Classic Piano Trio: Elmar Oliveira (violin); Peter Basquin (piano) This second of Schubert's piano trios is a long work and one of the great chamber compositions in this famous nineteenth-century composer's oeuvre. Schubert used a canon as the basis of his brilliant scherzo.

SCHUMANN Concerto for Violoncello and Orchestra in A minor, op. 129; Romantic Concert Pieces for 'Cello and Piano   MMOCD3705

CONCERTO: Vladimir Babbin (violoncello); Stuttgart Symphony Orchestra/Kahn; CONCERT PIECES: Kate Dillingham (violoncello) Linda Kessler-Ferri (piano) Schumann's concerto for violoncello, written in 1850, is one of the great pieces for this instrument. Schumann cast this piece (which he called a "concert-piece") in connected movements which give it an almost fantasia-like character. The accompanying concert pieces on this album are gems of the romantic repertoire. Glorious music!

Schumann Violoncello Concerto in A minor, op. 129; **Saint-Saëns** Carnival des Animaux (Carnival of the Animals): La Cygne (The Swan) (arr. for 'cello & piano); **Fauré (transcr. Pablo Casals)** Après un Rêve (arr. for 'cello & piano); **Mendelssohn** Song Without Words in D major, op. 109 (arr. for 'cello & piano)

SCHUMANN Piano Trio in D minor, op. 63   MMOCD3709

David Miller (violoncello) - The Classic Piano Trio: Elmar Oliveira (violin); Peter Basquin (piano) The Schumann Piano Trio is justly famous and provides numerous opportunities for the violoncello. Really a magnificent piece of music and important for every 'cellist to learn.

Ten Concert Pieces for Violoncello and Piano   MMOCD3704

Kate Dillingham (violoncello) - Linda Kessler-Ferri (piano) A wonderful group of pieces for 'cello and piano, this is one of the most popular violoncello albums in the MMO catalogue. Delightful music from a broad-ranging repertoire.

J.S. Bach (rev. Pablo Casals) Toccata in C major (Adagio); **Bloch (ed. Hans Kindler)** Jewish Life, No. 1: Prayer; **Davidov (ed. Leonard Rose)** At the Fountain, op. 20, no. 2; **Fauré (transcr. Pablo Casals)** Après un Rêve (arr. for 'cello & piano); **Granados (transcr. Gregor Piatigorsky)** Spanish Dances, op. 37, H142: 2. Oriéntale; **Mendelssohn** Song Without Words in D major, op. 109 (arr. for 'cello & piano); **Ravel** Pièce en Forme de Habanera; **Saint-Saëns** Allegro Appassionato in B minor for Violoncello & Orchestra, op. 43 (arrangement for 'cello & piano); Carnaval des Animaux (Carnival of the Animals): La Cygne (The Swan) (arr. for 'cello & piano); **Schumann** Phantasiestücke, op. 73: 1. 'Zart und mit Ausdruck' (arrangement for 'cello & piano)

WINER Violoncello Concerto; SCHUBERT Ave Maria; SAINT-SAENS Allegro Appassionato (pop ver.)   MMOCD3716

Steven Thomas (violoncello) - (orchestral accompaniment) New composer Ethan Winer's concerto is bursting with bold ideas and fresh orchestration; the album also contains a chamber-music version of Schubert's 'Ave Maria' and an energetic pop-orchestrated version of Saint-Saens' *Allegro Apassionata*--this album presents an exciting synthesis of modern-day and Romantic-era compositional ideas.

Ethan Winer Violoncello Concerto; **Schubert** Ellens Gesang III: 'Ave Maria', op. 52, no. 6 (arrangement for solo instrument with chamber ensemble); **Saint-Saëns, Camille (arr. Winer, Ethan)** Allegro Appassionato ('Insaen' pop version), op. 43

For our full catalogue, including more popular and jazz titles, classical concerti, chamber works and master classes for all instruments visit us on the web at

www.musicminusone.com

Call 1-800 669-7464 in the USA • 914 592-1188 International • Fax: 914 592-2751 email: info@musicminusone.com

MUSIC MINUS ONE
50 Executive Boulevard
Elmsford, New York 10523-4325
1.800.669.7464 U.S. ← 914.592.1188 International

www.musicminusone.com
mmogroup@musicminusone.com

MMO 3703   Pub. No. 0855   Printed in Canada